The Nature of Man

The Nature *of* Man

Poetry of Earth's Flora, Fauna, and the Human Condition

John L. Breska

RESOURCE *Publications* · Eugene, Oregon

THE NATURE OF MAN
Poetry of Earth's Flora, Fauna, and the Human Condition

Copyright © 2022 John L. Breska. All rights reserved. Except for brief quotations in critical publications or reviews, no part of this book may be reproduced in any manner without prior written permission from the publisher. Write: Permissions, Wipf and Stock Publishers, 199 W. 8th Ave., Suite 3, Eugene, OR 97401.

Resource Publications
An Imprint of Wipf and Stock Publishers
199 W. 8th Ave., Suite 3
Eugene, OR 97401

www.wipfandstock.com

PAPERBACK ISBN: 978-1-6667-3857-5
HARDCOVER ISBN: 978-1-6667-9945-3
EBOOK ISBN: 978-1-6667-9946-0

MARCH 16, 2022 8:42 AM

To GOD, Almighty!
To my grandsons, Layne, Carter, Anthony, Dallas, Angelo, Anderson, and Jackson.

Contents

Acknowledgement | xi

Introduction | xiii

When Old Men Gather | 1
Autumn Over the Berkshires | 2
Personal Laundry | 3
Eyedrops for the Soul | 3
Marshland Portrait | 4
The Visit | 5
In the Forest Green | 6
Leaving Summer | 7
Prayer for the Positive Path | 7
There Once Was a Hill | 8
Nature's Balance | 9
Autumn Morning | 9
Freedom | 10
Wind | 11
Of Loss | 11
Amphibian Perspective | 12
Late Autumn Child | 13
Winter Portrait #3 | 13
The Learning Tree | 14
A Natural Moment | 15
At a Turtle's Pace | 16

It's All in the Eyes | 17
Feather Philosophy | 18
Elk Story | 19
I Trusted You | 20
Along the Ausable | 21
The Fox | 22
Arizona Rock | 23
A Basket Full of Dreams | 24
The Humpback Whale | 25
Twilight | 26
Eulogy for a Rose | 27
For the Knowing | 28
The Gift | 29
The Red–Tailed Hawk | 30
Prayer from a Weary Soul | 31
The Apple | 32
The Goodness That Was Them | 32
The Mouse | 33
Barefoot Girl in a White Cotton Dress | 34
Hands | 35
The Foot | 35
Letter to Youth | 36
The Owl | 37
Chapel Pond | 38
Cow | 39
The Razor's Edge | 40
The Wonder of a Tree | 41
Ship of Fools | 42
Terrestrial Gastropod | 43
My Father's Barn | 44
An American Remembrance | 45
Gradualism of Love | 45

Butterfly (a daughter's growth) | 46
Old Fences | 47
A Moth in Love | 48
First Frost | 48
A Flower's Prayer | 49
Of Spring | 50
Deserted Farm | 51
My Father | 52
Wisconsin | 53
The Angler | 54
In Between | 55
Garden Guest | 57
Mouse Dreams | 58
Squirrels | 59
The Journey | 60
The Cricket's Band | 61
The Bird Feeder | 62
The Painted Horse | 63
The Pond | 64
Whales | 66
Colors (the loss of someone) | 67
Hope | 67
The Quenching (circa 1736) | 68
The Buck | 69
Wayside | 70
Saguaro | 71
What Bugs Me | 72
The Mountain | 73
To My Son | 74
Stone | 75
Leaf Thoughts | 76
The Farmer's Blessing | 77

The Tree | 78
As You Mourn | 79
Disease | 79
Tales of the Woods | 80
Early Evening Prayers | 81
Being Thankful | 81
Fresh Snow | 82
Adaptation | 82
Autumn on the Wind | 83
This Alaskan Way | 84
For Those Left Behind | 85
Quiet Times | 85
Rhythm of Life | 86
The Teacher | 87
Drifting | 88
Why We Sing | 89
The Fan | 89
Through the Rabbit's Eyes | 90
Remembering Gratitude | 91
Mississippi Portrait | 92
Divorce | 93
If Man Would Pray | 94
Sister | 95
The Understanding | 96
Art of Forgiving | 96
The Race | 97
A Song | 97
Grandpa | 98
Shine | 100

Acknowledgement

I'd like to thank my wife, Deborah Breska for creating
her original watercolor art for the cover,
as well as her love and support.

Additional thanks to my sister Judy,
for the second set of eyes on this work.

Introduction

I HAVE HAD THE PLEASURE of living in three areas of the United States during my lifetime. I enjoyed a nice childhood and spent my first thirty-seven years in Wisconsin. My job in the magazine printing industry afforded me an opportunity to relocate with my company out East in nineteen eighty-seven. I lived in Saratoga Springs, New York for the next twenty-two years and eventually finished my thirty-year career with Quad/Graphics, a Wisconsin based printer, in two-thousand nine. This opened the door for a new adventure where my wife, and I, retired to Mississippi until two-thousand fifteen. Late September of that year, we moved back to Wisconsin.

Having had an opportunity to see various patches of our country, I was inspired to write about a variety of fauna and flora which I encountered over the years. As with any journey, we are also blessed to meet souls along the way who give light to life or cloud the skies with their negativity. In all, I believe there are lessons brought to us in each case to educate the soul with.

I have written a couple thousand of pieces of poetry in my lifetime. Some, I would think are worth the time to digest, while others were less than worthy and found left on the plate, late after dinner. I have compiled a grouping that I would deem edible. It is my hope that you will enjoy the meal.

When Old Men Gather

Questioning the way things are, have always been my way,
I look, then wonder what about those things I see each day,
I ponder on the old men as they gather in the morn,
to share their many thoughts regarding every great storm

I look, as people concentrate on things which bring them down,
instead of looking for the light to see the good around,
for though our world is blemished by unbalance, hate and war,
we need to look beyond that page for truly there is more

Seasons seem to be there for a purpose set in time,
completion of the task brings due another cup of wine
and so, our lives are measured as we move along my friend,
see, nothing lasts forever, each new season has its end

I feel that someday all the world will be a better place
and sunshine will pour forth from all the souls we come to face,
then when the old men gather in the early morning light,
they'll talk about the heavens for the storm has passed at night

Autumn Over the Berkshires

The names gave not the colors worth, for what my eyes could see,
as earth tones graced the leaves that hung, so gracious from each tree
and I was left in total awe at GOD's artistic hand,
thus, overcome with gratitude, I wept upon the land

Burnt umber, red, orange, yellow partings, drifted down to earth,
a melancholy attitude of autumn giving birth,
suspended right between the ground and heaven's endless space,
a mist hung on the mountain as a veil on a face

I drew a breath both deep and long while witnessing the view,
'twas then that I became aware of things I thought I knew,
I heard an angel singing a cappella from above,
places in my heart spilled over with eternal love

If I were blessed to hold this feeling for one second more,
I do believe I'd die of joy and to the heavens soar,
for beauty such as this, I don't believe I've ever known,
that morning I looked through God's eye and saw a glimpse of home

Personal Laundry

There's a therapeutic value in the folding of one's clothes
that I find here, in the laundromat today,
for my mind begins revealing things that everybody knows
but could never find it in their hearts to say

It is me that needed washing, from my mind down to my soul,
for my thinking had been soiled and quite stained,
all those years of mere existence left a void; an endless hole
and the only time I'd cry is when it rained

Now, my soap is new ideas, for I'm cleaning up my act,
need a lot of fabric softener, you see,
lining all my seams together, smoothing wrinkles with much tact
and I'm finding there's a brighter, cleaner me

Eyedrops for the Soul

When I'm perplexed about the day, I find a quiet place
and let the angels gather 'round to sooth my twisted face,
I close my eyes then clear my head to quell the endless noise
and in a stretch of time, I'm sure to find my inner poise

I cleanse the palate of the soul by spitting out the bones,
I lighten up my burden by removing many stones
and when the sunset paints the clouds in pastels overhead,
I know I'll sleep a peaceful sleep when my head finds the bed

Marshland Portrait

Cattails rise from earth toward sky,
all lifeless now,
brown stalks stand tall,
ice holds them stationary
as they mark the pond beneath

Solo finch lands on shaft,
sways endlessly,
looks everywhere,
as snow dust falls around her
from its resting place atop

Underneath the silt and mud,
old turtles dream
through winter's dance,
subzero days above them,
mixed with snowfall, sleet, and arctic wind

Resting through those long cold months,
are many forms
of life asleep,
awaiting spring's warm welcome,
meanwhile February reigns

Final, thoughtful, portrait shows
a field mouse,
near grassy tuft,
preparing his quick journey
over frozen waterways
to a warm nest

The Visit

Through the morning mist I spy,
a solo angel passing by
and as I start to say hello,
it turns to me and smiles, you know

A peaceful, quite angelic smile
and I am mesmerized a while,
no words are ever shared or said
but spirits weave a tender web

And I see glimpses past man's eye,
to places far beyond our sky
and yet they parallel with earth,
while passing on, is just new birth

Where we are shown eternity
and sights we thought we'd never see,
amazing things beyond man's scope,
where sits the origin of hope

Where faith was born to every man
and love was always in the plan,
the angel thus nods gracefully,
then fades far past reality

I stand there speechless for a time,
as I breathe deep, a living sign,
I ponder over what occurred,
remembering without one word

That there is more to what we know,
that heaven waits beyond life's glow,
that we were sent to find our way,
back to GOD's pure love someday

In the Forest Green

I search for solace in the forest green,
where man and nature share the seeker's dream,
a place of sounds quite natural to all,
where listening brings wonder without shout or call

I see that time leaves markers far and near,
moss covered stump where stood a giant fir,
new acorn shoots that rooted in the spring,
horned owl's nesting chicks, in dead tree trunk, standing

The song of water running through the banks
gives me a sense of life and giving thanks,
whitetail deer stop for a needed drink,
alert to any sound, for danger's on the brink

Clear my many worries under canopy,
scolded by the red squirrels for the likes of me,
after my devotions I'll be on my way,
leaving the forest as it was this very day

Leaving Summer

The early leaves of autumn's fall have drifted down
and rest upon the farmer's pond, a time,
while colors change throughout the land,
a late September sign

The geese honk overhead as wedges fly due south
and sandhill cranes not far behind, retreat,
much cooler nights do grace our sleep,
as autumn comes to greet

The squirrels begin to bury food for harder times,
while ravens caw a signal for their friends,
pumpkin crop turns orange from green,
as summer slowly ends

Prayer for the Positive Path

May your life be filled with the opportunity
to heal a moment in the fabric of time,
to help, rather than hinder,
to create, instead of destroy
and in one thousand years,
no one will remember
other than the LORD,
that you were a positive
in a world of negativity
and you brought light to a darkened day

There Once Was a Hill

The hill behind the old farmhouse gave me eyes to see,
that there was a much larger world with less serenity,
some days I'd sit there watching clouds of varied shapes go by,
or lean against an old oak tree and simply wonder why

Somedays, I'd spend an afternoon with friends from down the road,
or sit with Mother Nature's friends; the squirrel, the jay, the toad,
long hours spent in thought about the coming county fair
and if I'd get a ribbon for a calf that I took there

I hid out when I crossed my Pa for things he called a sin,
then slunk home nearer dinner time, my Ma's voice on the wind,
the farm looked awful small from there, where I felt I was king
and in my adolescent voice that cracked, I'd try to sing

When Pa passed on, I climbed the hill and sat until sunset,
I thought of all he taught me as most silently I wept,
the farm was sold some years ago and Ma moved into town,
it hurt to lose my childhood perch and to this day I frown

A subdivision clutters up the land that I called mine,
but so it goes with many things that fall behind the time,
sometimes I drive up on the hill where many people live,
a tender place I shared with GOD, where GOD taught me to give

Nature's Balance

Tears of the mountain's melting snow,
stream down its face to the valley below,
quenching the fields who thirst just to grow,
in sunlit days of summer

Fears of the farmer find their way,
thinking of drought on an August day,
hoping the rains come to dance and play,
ear tuned to heaven's thunder

Some years the flooding takes its toll,
rain drowns the earth like it has no soul,
balance in nature the only goal,
time marks our wait and wonder

Autumn Morning

October geese sound overhead
as dreams escape my once warm bed,
first finch arrives for thistle seed,
fulfilling life's most basic need

I watch the progress of the dawn,
escapes, an almost thoughtless yawn,
a solitary doe appears,
she pauses as she lifts her ears

Eyes wide, she moves behind the trees,
softly away by autumn's breeze,
clear pearls of dew on spider's lace,
a portrait of this morning's face

I weigh and reason all I see,
then pen it, for the life of me

Freedom

We gathered by the shores of freedom
one cold winter day,
someone rang a bell amongst us
then said, "Let us pray,"
we prayed for every fallen soul,
who lost their life in each war's toll,
we voiced their names against drum roll,
then slowly walked away

I found a snowy knoll behind me
where I stood in thought,
thinking that the price of freedom
can't be cheaply bought,
remembering the battles well,
of fields turned to living hell,
I filled with tears until tears fell,
on land where wars were fought

I looked beyond the frozen waters
far across the earth,
life took on a different picture
still, a common birth,
I looked within and wondered why,
how all could live beneath one sky
and never quite see eye to eye,
on GOD, on life, on worth

The bell rang in the distance, calling
as I turned about,
breathing in, I knew my colors
and there was no doubt,
freedom's shore was mine to hold,
through the heat and through the cold,
call me brassy, call me bold,
but "Freedom" was my shout

Wind

I love to see the wind in dance with the trees across the land,
no angered wind which destroys and hurts
but a wind caressing, that inserts,
a wind that merrily winds through the branches swaying to and fro,
a most pleasant wind which ruffles hairs, a wind that both will come and
go
an invisible but friend of mine who whispers on the breeze,
when it tires from the dancing with the tall and awesome trees,
then the sun sets quietly near night and the wind fades soft, with ease

Of Loss

Tend the brokenhearted as they grieve,
for tears of loss weigh heavy on one's sleeve
and though we feel like all is lost we find the path again,
thus, over time one heals some, while GOD removes the pain

Amphibian Perspective

Cold air over early morning lake
brings a mist to light,
which adds mystique across surrounding lowlands,
weathered dock sits crippled from the shoreline
out into the shallows,
heavy slant, with wooden boat
haphazardly tied fore and aft

A dragonfly is plucked from surface water
causing brief disruption,
then calm returns to dawn's awakening,
a pair of mallards glide between the reeds
like skaters on a winter pond,
poetic, as they parallel each other's moves

Protruding eyes
assess the foreground,
making sure no heron lurks
along the banks nor in those algae laden pools,
that form beneath the willows hanging down

When considered safe,
a lone frog sounds,
calling to all that would care
and sounders answer to each other
that they are aware

Late Autumn Child

The north wind blows reminders
that winter's on its way
and I, much like the grasshopper,
continue with my play

The leaves dance all around me,
I frolic here and there,
then suddenly, I look around,
for something's in the air

I smell the fields resting,
for harvest is complete,
the barn is full, the cupboard stocked
and warmth awaits retreat

Hypnotic is the fire
that brings the hearth aglow,
"goodnight late autumn hours spent,
time to rest you know"

Winter Portrait #3

Winter sun pierces the icicle
throwing its glare
through the stalactite,
like some constant changing prism
as it melts into a watery drip

Solidifying its remains
as the daylight ends
and the temperature drops,
holding motion to a standstill once again

The Learning Tree

I wandered through a forest simply lost in my direction
and found a small, odd clearing, with a solitary tree,
I took a closer look, for it was strange on my inspection,
with variety of fruits of which no names would come to me

Quite hungry from meandering, I picked a colored bauble,
within a bite or maybe two, I felt enlightenment,
on finishing, I picked a second orb but for my trouble,
that when consuming it, I seemed quite humbled when it spent

I rested underneath its branches falling in deep slumber,
I dreamt as I ate each new fruit, an attribute so attained
and thus, I gorged myself to where I lost digested number,
while stomach ached for taking in more any man had gained

When I awoke, I understood we all are blessed a portion,
while too much of just anything will often turn to waste,
we're given steps along the way, each one proceeds a notion,
for man is balanced in his life where all should get a taste

I understood I had my fill though tempted, I resisted,
my time had passed, and I knew I should be fast, on my way,
for something told me, had I stayed and greedily persisted,
too much of a good thing might bring me where I'd gone astray

A Natural Moment

An early morning doe appeared,
she offered me a look,
we shared the daybreak
for a bit,
her eyes on me
and I, on her

And then without a single word,
she jumped the living brook,
and for her own sake
did not sit,
but chose to flee,
to disappear

Perhaps the safety of the herd
is why to flight she took,
and as for my take,
I was fit,
to watch with glee,
to be so near

Sweet moments that life has incurred
would fill a poet's book,
heart and soul would ache
without it,
GOD's works to see,
all I find dear

At a Turtle's Pace

Patches of shade and sunlight,
intermingled over winding road
and I, a solitary traveler
walking beneath this canopy of forest,
like a fish who swims the ocean
on a partly cloudy day

My canvas alters color as I go

These silhouettes and brilliant shapes,
created by attendant leaves and branches,
which share the space above,
find harmony while bathed by solar rays
and washed again on other days
by steady, falling rain

These are fond awarenesses
and I am but a journalist
within the confines of an active mind,
here to note those gifts
that somehow fall between life's busy pace,
that turtles seldom know

Perhaps we search
for that which we already have in tow,
but cannot see simplicity
within our complex lives,
for in our quest to get ahead,
we leave the dock without a boat to row

It's All in the Eyes

In my grandmother's eyes there are stories,
of the hours that changed into days, into years,
of the joys and the sorrows, the laughter, and tears,
of the peace that she found and the worries

In my grandfather's eyes are the trails,
in the building, and fixing, and working his days,
in the cuts and the wrinkles and scars, he displays,
in a lifetime of hammers and nails

In my young, grandson's eyes, are life's future,
as he plays and he watches, and learns as he goes,
as he practices skills that so proudly, he shows,
as he grows from a student to teacher

In my own son's eyes are his reflection,
from a place I had been just a sunrise before,
from a youthful exuberance at the front door,
from a life that was full of selection

In my own eyes the mirror shows yearning,
there were distances walked in the sunsets I've known,
there were falsehoods and wisdom found under each stone,
there was calm in between all the churning

Feather Philosophy

A sparrow falls to earth
unnoticed by its silenced song,
while time and man
continue on their way,
too busy as they play

No more, no less,
a flower of the field,
that has faltered under sky
and one we have to say goodbye,
for each of us must die

In quiet,
we are left to wonder
where our wings will cease,
and cause us
to relinquish flight,
abruptly, day or night

Peace be mine
for understanding,
there is nothing
to be done,
but living out the moments GOD has given,
content to know,
I am another sparrow

Elk Story

The Shawnee named them Wapiti,
large, red deer of the Eastern Rockies,
antlers reaching toward the stars,
commanding presence, silhouetted against a rose hued sunset

Folklore tells the tale of the great one on a ridge,
who raised his head with rack,
then punctured clouds

Rains fell,
ending winter, bringing spring,
new calves were born,
the herd grew,
where they grazed among the aspen and the conifers

Forward, through the grassy foothills,
searching for new dandelions,
clover, and sweet violets in bloom,
the cows found fine surroundings,
while the bulls watched from the knolls
and life was good, for yet another season

I Trusted You

When I let you hold the candle in that darkest place,
when I let you take your hand and gently touch my face,
when I feared and held you close
I thought you really knew,
that of all GOD's living things
I trusted you

When I let you see me crying, while my guard was down,
when I shared my many dreams that never left the ground,
when I lost my will to live
for sadness turned me blue,
you were where I always turned,
I trusted you

When the north wind tried to part us, didn't I hold on,
when sharing something special, you were the only one,
when I opened up my soul
to show exactly who
I was, because it's you I loved,
I trusted you

When you said you needed time, I took the clocks away,
when I asked for truth, you told me stories every day,
when you said, "Forever More"
upon a time once true,
this fool believed, for through it all,
I trusted you

Along the Ausable

Smoke ascends high through the pines,
I weigh what's yours,
I weigh what's mine,
I look around at everything,
the fallen limbs,
fresh shoots of spring

Waters flow 'long side the camp
and for this time,
I am a tramp,
I walk the riverbank all day
and without form,
I find I pray

As early evening settles in,
the loon calls out
while I listen,
I stir the fire, add a log,
far through the trees,
I hear a dog

Resurrection of the night,
the stars return,
I watch this sight,
sweet wonder captivates the man,
of all of this,
I'm glad I am

The Fox

Wandering fox on a late winter day,
nose on the ground,
ears perked for sound,
scavenging edibles, making his way,
searching the snow,
for food, you know

Eyes move about as the chickadees sing,
paused, for a time,
then on to dine,
visions of pheasant eggs from the past spring,
perhaps a mouse,
far from his house

Slipping along the backside of a barn,
looking to see,
what there might be,
sun starts to set as he combs through the farm,
little for him,
pickins are slim

Rust coat and tail both tipped off in black,
moves down the road,
towards his abode,
comes a new dawn, he will surely be back,
seeking to break,
that hunger ache

Arizona Rock

Dry wind blow gently past my face
and share your news of life beyond this place,
for I have sat here patiently
while years have passed,
as sands of time fell free,
for I have been a rock
as you can see

Sweet rain, please wash my body clean,
to ease the heat that never ends this dream
and may a cloud block the sunshine,
to help me last,
to shade me while I pine,
for I have been a rock
throughout all time

Dear night, be filled with stars for me,
that I may look to heaven's endless sea,
a comfort that will ease my pain,
as I've been left
upon this desert plain,
for I have been a rock
and that's my fame

New dawn, bring change to what I've known,
perhaps a boulder or a smaller stone,
another that might know my song
and share my day,
no matter right or wrong,
for I have been a rock
so very long

A Basket Full of Dreams

We each compile over time, a basket full of dreams,
I wonder Mother, if your dreams came true,
I hope that they included washing tee shirts, socks, and jeans,
as well as tending measles and the flu

I guess I just forget about the hours that you kept
in raising both my sister and myself,
the lunches that you packed for Dad while everybody slept,
then groceries from store to cupboard shelf

I'm asking if there was some joy for you in all of this,
in retrospect, it was a lot of work,
perhaps it came when we were small and shared a goodnight kiss,
here's hoping that was not your only perk

I wish I'd been a better son and somehow made you proud,
my heart was always in that certain place
but trouble seemed to follow like the old symbolic cloud
and I'd come home with mud upon my face

We're older now and dreams are few, for wants and needs are less,
I'm happy just to rise up each new morn,
you need to know I love you and I pray that GOD will bless
and thanks for being there when I was born

The Humpback Whale

Magnificent mountain, it breaches the surface,
the water explodes and it rains for a while,
I'm caught by this vision for no other purpose,
than given to stare with great awe at such style

A ballet of humpbacks adds poise to the ocean,
their tails most elegant, arced in the air,
a portrait of grace in perpetual motion,
they move through their days without nary a care

The blue light of evening sets mood to performance,
their song bids a welcome to all living things,
for they live each day as if life were true romance,
an attitude, living in love often brings

Twilight

The pages of both day and night
share in transition's world,
an essence changing all we see
from hard life to a softened state,
a glow is painted on the clouds,
reflective moods on mountain peaks,
the heavens rest in awesome shades of
purples, mauve and fire orange

Life's edges muted for a bit
where wind stops just to sigh,
the sun rests easy in this space,
the moon approaches slow
and in these moments, there's a pause,
that somehow soothes us all,
those few shared beats among the dark and light

So, I am left to twilight's time,
my eyes take sight of all that's shown,
the inner me digests the mood
that's somewhere in between,
while I'm content to stay awake
inside this living dream

Eulogy for a Rose

What purpose served that flowers die,
I ask this for I need to know,
why once it stood, bright life, full glow,
but now it withers so

The red rose turns and sad am I,
it darkens to a purple shade,
the leaves, bright green, begin to fade,
the stem, limp, without aid

It brings this man to almost cry,
for vision comes and I can see,
that life's full circle sets one free,
rose knows eternity

The truth is never one to lie,
my vision tells me rose has gone,
but I still hear the flower's song,
her scent remains, so long

For the Knowing

The distance between here and there might shorten with a certain phrase,
then misconceptions dissipate like smoke beyond our being
and pain once felt, melts like the snows when sun shines down its praise,
'tis healing that comes, dear to us, much like the blind start seeing

Old pain is lost by efforts made to find a mending of the heart
but motion must be put in gear to change our way of dealing,
for if we only wish that day, the day will never come take part
and old hurt festers over time, a cancer that we're feeling

Don't salt those wounds, they're lessons taught, we learn and graduate in time,
it's part of being part of life to understand we're growing,
so, let go of those hurts and pain, you'll feel an inner shine,
then make the first move, make amends, and be blessed for the knowing

The Gift

I watched a yellow daffodil come slowly into being,
it opened in great gratitude beneath a winter sun
and for the first time in a long time, I was blessed in seeing,
the gift of life that touches everyone

I thought of how a mother cries at her first born's arrival,
for nothing is as beautiful as being part of birth
and as the child clings to her, in fact, for its survival,
envisioned is a picture of self–worth

I guess it is that way with men who build on new conception,
creation of a single thought; the flame that lights the way,
perhaps they nurture it to life and hope for its perfection,
within man's private garden, comes what may

I read the road I travel on, my pace is somewhat slower,
I'm learning how to make the most of every new dawn,
for something has awaked me, as sun upon the flower,
yet flowers bloom so briefly, then they're gone

The Red–Tailed Hawk

As quiet as the clouds on high,
the silent watcher glides on by,
engaged in hunting from the sky,
her eye upon the slightest sigh

She floats upon the wind, so free,
sometimes, I wish that I were she,
true visions from the air, to see,
as GOD might ponder over me

I'm awed by her born, natural grace,
determination on her face,
magnificent, she floats in space,
for here, is where she sets her pace

A new sun comes to let her know,
that wind beneath the wings should flow
and unknown to the game below,
the hunt goes on, for life is so

Prayer from a Weary Soul

Hear my cry O' Light Divine,
for I am at the place where people find their knees,
my spirit staggers as I sift the ashes of my mind
and embers that once burned with heart, I can no longer find,
I walk the endless forest but I cannot see the trees,
Your help would be a blessing and accepted at this time

Understand my plea is real,
for I'm not one to quibble over things so trite
but would so solve the problem if I had the means at hand,
You've placed it in my nature to be one to take a stand
but I've known moments that have simply blinded my good sight
and I no longer have the means to process what I feel

Comfort me, in all You are,
for all is overwhelming and I need Your grace,
take me, who knows the secret that in You I truly live
and show Yourself, that I may come to grips and then forgive
myself and all the times I fell upon this human face,
for then I'll know there is no near nor far

The Apple

What truer beauty shall we see,
than one fresh apple from a tree,
that glistens in the day's bright sun,
a deep, red ruby when it's done

Oh, tender morsel that we find,
a sphere of health for all mankind,
which gives us pleasure to consume,
at dawn, midday or nighttime's moon

What was it that old Newton said,
when one lone apple hit his head,
I think before he bat an eye,
his vision was of apple pie

The Goodness That Was Them

The sands of time pass through the narrows
but stop not for man nor woman
and we who come into this life from the miracle of birth,
leave shortly after our arrival

Where they walked and talked and were
are places where they cease to be,
but still are felt among us,
marking hearts, for the goodness that was them

The Mouse

Tiny tracks upon the snow,
barely visible, you know,
early morning traveler,
in search of grains and berries

Through a small crack in the barn,
staying clear of every harm,
one quick, tiny, ball of fur,
who dreams of cheese and cherries

On the shelf above its head,
someone's dropped a piece of bread,
snatch it fast, in one small blur
and solve this morning's worries

Little eyes look left, then right,
small nose sniffs the air in fright,
false alarm but best be sure,
as this one darts and scurries

Back to filling up thy needs,
cracking wheat and barley seeds,
breakfast solved now, as it were,
it's home before snow flurries

Barefoot Girl in a White Cotton Dress

She looks for shells along the shore, examining each one,
she puts them close to ear then listens deeply till they're done
but comes the time when she must set each shell back in the sand,
for there are more shells down the beach that she must give a hand

She searches for some sign that oceans hold a bit of truth,
which reaches back to places when the rocks remembered youth,
she gathers bits of wisdom from the song that whales sing,
in order that she understands what life has yet to bring

She looks beyond the breakers where the sea and sun meet late,
thoughts drift upon the waters as her way to contemplate,
the meaning of the nature and the order of life's ways,
she measures in beginnings and those endings of the days

She finds a comfort in the washing of the edge of land,
as waves move over footsteps where she does no longer stand,
pure innocence that ballets down the long and winding coast,
for love of GOD resides within this ever–loving host

Hands

On all there is to understand
one needs to get a grip,
to grasp the concept of the hand
from wrist to very tip,
four fingers and the distanced thumb
has language of its own,
those nails, knuckles and a palm
can halt or wave you home

Can ball up in a mighty fist
or open as a friend,
can guide and possibly assist,
receive something or send,
communicate by using sign,
indicate what's yours and mine,
hold the moment, spill the wine,
give or take away the time

We're given pairs to clasp in prayer
or clap in joyful bliss,
but I shall always be aware
of hands I've come to miss

The Foot

I stand in awe with regards to feet;
supporting characters,
a pedestal for each man to meet
the day as it occurs

A sole, five toes and a heel too
describes the normal foot,
designed as such to move all men through
life's roses and life's soot

Letter to Youth

Dear youth,
why has thou left so suddenly,
that I've been cursed to age before
reflections in the pond
and much like leaves fast falling from a tree,
I see life's season ending, just beyond

Dear youth,
where have you gone to play your games,
I sit alone, I ponder on
the passing suns and moons
and now this one is filled with aches and pains,
where city stood, there's nothing left but ruins

Dear youth,
what flagrant joke have you brought forth,
that has me crying, hence, the punch
line humors me no more
and I am feeling less than my self-worth,
for yonder, goes said youth, right out the door

The Owl

Indifference sits high above the ground,
she watches patiently without a sound,
prepared to land like Dorothy's house,
hard, on a rabbit or a mouse,
a raptor contemplating life's invasion

Nocturnal aviator blinks her eyes,
as if to say, "This wait is no surprise,"
she'll take whatever comes along,
for nature only knows one song,
the lesson being, "Chance rights the equation"

The honor of false wisdom finds its way,
bestowed upon this ancient bird of prey,
who only wishes solitude,
at risk of being somewhat rude,
inviting one to lunch, takes clawed persuasion

Chapel Pond

When the light eludes me
and I am left to my own kind,
I know just where the angels go,
I wander there and don't you know,
they never really mind

High upon the rock face
we sit among the aspen trees,
and share the peace of everything,
as faith and hope begin to sing,
then ride the ancient breeze

Mirrored thing of beauty
at mountain base and just beyond,
I gaze at your reflective eye,
it looks back and it's me I spy,
above old Chapel Pond

'Tis my sanctuary
here, among celestial wings,
I come to find myself again,
and all is well, there is no pain,
perspective straightens things

Soul, with inspiration,
it brings me back and I am found,
I bid the angels fond adieu,
they smile on with spirits true
and life's a pleasant sound

Cow

Complacency upon four hooves,
rhythm in the chew,
landlocked to an area,
seldom shows hysteria,
calm, collective,
most serene,
in the meadow by the stream,
Guernsey, Brown Swiss or Holstein,
udderly benign,
readily bovine

Stands at ease in sisterhood,
partnership that's sealed,
bringing to the farmer's table,
every day, their yield,
each, a painted work of art,
big warm eyes that melt the heart,
sunrise has them all take part,
these experts in their field

The Razor's Edge

There's a point in time where one decides the path they travel on,
real life eludes the troubled man, from sunset until dawn,
he seeks a higher wisdom as he searches for the truth
but questions deep inside him, keep the answers much aloof

He looks for inspiration on a foreign mountain peak
and he turns to an old, wise man for the truth that all men seek,
the old man says to ponder on the values of mankind,
then chants a holy mantra, giving praise to soul and mind

Now the seeker prays for GOD's own word; Eternal Light Divine,
or visions from the heavens high, however small the sign,
he stands among the clouds in awe, feet planted on a ledge,
his life is balanced in the wind, upon a razor's edge

The spirit thrives inside this man who wonders who he is,
his willingness to search the world, his lasting eagerness,
he stops to drink and sees himself reflected in the pond,
thus recognizing finally where man and spirit bond

The Wonder of a Tree

Within the meadow stands a tree,
unique, with feelings I can see,
long branches reaching toward the sky,
as if to say, "I wonder why"

So rooted deep to hold its own,
to weather out the strongest storm,
so full of life, sweet buds in spring,
give cause for all the birds to sing

Sad loss of summer to its end
and leaves like tears fall from my friend,
this tree grows silent in the snow
and waits for winter's chill to go

Warm season comes, I rest my head,
against its trunk, I make my bed,
the wind on meadow dances through,
while tree and I, we both stay true

Appreciating I for me
and I return love to this tree,
the days all pass like clouds on high,
and often we both wonder why

Ship of Fools

A ship of many sails boasted, "On the waves, the best!"
and none could go the distance, he was faster than the rest,
he touted on his own behalf the measure of his worth,
from stern to bow he raved his value since his shipyard birth

"They'll someday write a song about my exploits, rest assured
and all will know what I've believed without another word,
immortalized, I'll truly be, in ports around the world,
my colors will fly from my mast in open breeze, unfurled"

So, on it went, the boasting and the bragging everyday
and all that tried to race the ship, outsailed, as they say,
until one stormy night where wind and storm had heard their fill,
feeling that a lesson learned might humble, if you will

The ship was tossed much like a cork on curls both great and small
and when the elements eased up, much water filled the hull,
an irreversible life change started to take form,
the ship began to sink below and thus was moved to mourn

As it drew closer to the bottom of the endless sea,
it thought, "There's many ships down here who were once, fast as me,
it seems that in my urge to be the best, I've sprung a leak
and found the place where ego rests when we are so unique"

Terrestrial Gastropod

Behold the garden slug,
an unprotected entity,
that moves across both nature's rug
and climbs the flowers forestry

A slow examiner,
exposed to life, on life's own terms,
it glides along without a stir,
among the beetles, ants, and worms

So philosophical,
perhaps, in how it views its world,
an observationist, its call,
antennae in the air unfurled

At length, an oversight,
to us who have a higher seat
but to a bird in morning light,
an absolutely, tasty treat

My Father's Barn

Faint glimpses of times earlier
when this barn stood erect,
a giant on the open plain
demanding great respect

Bright red, with white trim all around,
so pleasing to the eye
and in our minds as children see,
believed it touched the sky

A place where we would run and play
a game of hide and seek,
a church of solace, in that barn,
for me, once every week

I sat up in the loft some days
while father worked the land
and more times than I wanted to,
I was the hired hand

I pass that barn from time to time,
it's weathered, worn and gray,
it leans and creaks of memories,
a song of yesterday

A hotel for the field mouse,
an owl on the wing,
a place for snow to land and sleep,
an old, but treasured thing

An American Remembrance

One feather fell from somewhere,
it drifted to the ground,
no notice or disturbance,
in fact, without a sound,
it landed on a peaceful night
with message quite profound,
that freedom was an endless flight
for eagles were around

Gradualism of Love

Love comes as an unforeseen moment of pleasure
then is tested in the fires of commitment,
taken further past the limits of our own agendas
to a place, where, if allowed,
will open worlds yet undiscovered,
and two souls can find a place called home

Butterfly (a daughter's growth)

I found a place of observation,
watched with wide-eyed wonder,
over time and contemplation
some days calm, some, thunder,
some days she was never seen,
some days woman, some days teen,
some days she would dance and preen
and some days she would blunder

A metaphoric transformation
almost disbelieving,
struggled long, to great elation,
joy mixed with some grieving

New life brings another view,
new life grows a wing or two,
new life makes the world anew,
for old lives we are leaving

Old Fences

Old fences have their memories,
they stand in fields where they once were trees,
so gently fondled by the summer breeze,
split, cracked and shifted by the winter freeze

Old fences always touch my heart,
I've come to know them as a work of art,
a post and rail at the very start,
which over time, quite prone to fall apart

Old fences help in many ways,
a home for field mice on rainy days,
a place for songbirds to enjoy sun rays,
a border for the farmer's many strays

Old fences have been good to me,
a place I've often found tranquility,
where I would write long lines of poetry,
they never kept me in, they always set me free

A Moth in Love

I see your flame aglow
on the canvas of the night,
it draws me near your side
for I am smitten by your love,
then I reach the place
where you are emanating from,
I feel the warmth,
hypnotically drawn,
yet, still remain upon the wing,
for deep, deep down
I feel surprise,
in the form of my demise

First Frost

October dawn awakens me
as dim light seeps through my windowpane,
I rise, I leave tranquility,
I stretch into reality,
then something catches both my eyes,
as autumn springs a cool surprise,
the field has a silver sheen
that's covered up once endless green,
first frost has come to stake its claim
while all growth stops its gain

A Flower's Prayer

Oh, gracious tears that fall toward earth,
you help each seed as it gives birth,
come land on me that I may grow,
my spirit withers so

Dear clouds so full, come rain on me,
come wash my leaves that I might be,
cry down on me and quench my thirst,
you find me at my worst

Sweet water that's been lifted high,
return to bless this soul who's nigh,
I cannot reach the sun alone,
I need you in my home

Run through the soil, to my roots,
come fill me and I'll grow new shoots,
you are the blood of life for all,
I pray you'll start to fall

Of Spring

Come the first few signs of spring,
snowdrops and the crocus bring,
blizzards changed to flowing streams,
winter but a dream, it seems

Come the colored birds up north,
singing songs of life and worth,
building nests in bush and tree,
dancing in the air, so free

Come the warming, sun filled rays,
length is given to our days,
faint reminders in the shade,
bits of snow that will not fade

Come forsythia to bloom,
underneath the first spring moon,
romance rises in the air,
new love blossoms everywhere

Come the time to grow again,
moving forward to remain,
part of everything we are,
seasoned, somewhere near and far

Deserted Farm

The wind blows easy from the north,
it moves the barn door back and forth,
the rusted hinges sing of times,
when milk cows filled the stalls

The silo moans a hollow song,
been void of silage for too long,
the barn boards, gray, and weathered signs,
that once made up the walls

Old fences settle to the ground,
they move toward earth, nary a sound,
except, the wind o'er barbed wire whines,
a death note as each falls

The farm's house, silent in its stance,
the wind examines rooms by chance,
no life is there, the wind, it pines,
then stillness, as it stalls

The lonely field's overgrown,
abandoned feelings set the tone,
utility pole with downed lines,
no matter, no one calls

My Father

I often think about my father who's been gone awhile
and how we seemed to always be abrasive in our style,
we saw things one time, eye to eye when I had reached his height
and though I loved him dearly, I saw black while he saw white

Much of this non-collaboration came from my own youth
and we each had opinions but that's why the voter's booth,
perhaps we both observed each other, finding parts insane
and in that, were discouraged, we both truly were the same

His birthday never passes without thoughts both good and bad
and how he found his end will always make me very sad,
his Christian name was Walter and I miss him tenderly
I wonder…if at times, he thinks about and misses me

Wisconsin

My home of birth still calls to me
though I've been gone for years,
the rolling hills, the wind so free,
the memories bring tears

The dairy farms all through the state,
the rivers, and the streams
and sunrise o'er that mighty lake,
gave birth to many dreams

I always felt a peace inside
while traveling the land,
for something warmer than just pride,
kept my heart close at hand

I've spent grand summers in the north
with family and friend,
I fell in love with natures worth,
through seasons, end to end

The red squirrel and the white tail deer,
the muskellunge, and loon,
enhance that place I see so clear,
that love, I'll visit soon

Wisconsin is the name she bears,
that place where I was born,
a lifetime journal my mind shares,
through fields of hay and corn

The Angler

In the early morning hours of a chilly April morn,
I rise quickly from the comfy bed where I laid safe and warm,
as the dawn makes known its presence, I look out to check the sky,
there are many open spaces where the blue has caught my eye

Tying flies, most days in winter, had anticipation soar,
I had mentally prepared myself for luck to be in store,
on the surface I could see the line that guided out the bait,
then feel the tug, next, set the hook, and visualize the plate

In the corner are my fly rod and my hip boots standing tall,
hat, and vest are calmly waiting on a peg just down the hall,
in the minutes that will follow, I'll be dressed and out the door,
heading north to the Ausable for sweet solitude and more

When a man stands in the river, there are thoughts that come and go,
when he looks upon the nature of the way the waters flow,
one cannot deny that GOD has had a very active hand,
in the building, and the forming of the beauty of this land

I'm surrounded by the mountains, in a place I call my home,
it's a garden on this planet where I've been allowed to roam,
where the black fly larva dance upon the avenue of fish,
where each man may catch his trophy and complete a lifelong wish

In Between

Like time spent after act one ends
and the set decorations change,
the second act hasn't started yet,
so, performers catch a smoke outside,
while others practice lines or rest
before the curtain call

This is how it is with me
when I am in between it all

Like nights that follow a full moon
when the glow dwindles down in size,
'til none remains, only darkness reigns,
with a modicum of stars above,
that place and time before new orb
grows in the heaven's womb

This is how it is with me
when I am in between each moon

Like those surviving failed love,
there's a time when we feel removed,
we're empty hearts in a heartless world,
it's a nomad's life in a barren land,
we wait for some sign to go on,
unnerved by quiet times

This is how it is with me
when I am in between the rhymes

This is how it is with me
when I am in between,
when a piece is finished
and I wake up from the dream,
when the trail cools
or I thirst and cannot find the stream

Given time I find my way,
to share the words another day

Garden Guest

Encounters of a hummingbird
passed on without a single word,
she stopped just inches from my face,
transfixed above my garden's space

She wasn't there then, there she was,
a faint but noticeable buzz,
she paused, then disappeared in flight,
in hope, I wished it was not fright

And so, it seems, this was my day
for she returned to have her way,
composure held, I did not blink,
not sure if I could even think

Eyes opened wide, we shared some time,
split seconds, then a quick beeline,
Monarda filled with nectar sweet,
could not be shunned, one special treat

Deep red blooms dancing in the air,
she partnered each with tender care,
a glance brought this bird back to me,
then gone, this small, winged mystery

Mouse Dreams

I rise up on my hind legs and I sniff the cool, spring air,
something whets my appetite,
some fine morsel, bite, I might,
something that's just out of sight
which needs direct attention

I start my search, exploring all the areas that fair,
underneath the farmer's door,
then inspect the kitchen floor,
crumbs greet me and nothing more,
but still, enough to mention

The cat sleeps in the corner as I dart by with great care,
down the baseboard's length I fly,
for to be caught, die, would I,
safe inside the pantry, sigh,
perhaps I'll see my pension

I'm closer to the source of food that's made me so aware,
in the cupboard I dart quick,
climbing shelves of one inch thick,
smell the cheese as lips I lick,
and then I feel the tension

A nice, sweet curd sits in the trap, and I am left to stare,
something says, "It's death to stay,
live to eat another day,"
tempted, but I steal away
escaping man's invention

Squirrels

Agile grays of northern states
remind me of lost acrobats,
who brag their skills before the world,
with confidence of fish in water,
they master every challenge
that would hold them from their destination,
puzzle solving like a scientist in study

Down the hedgerow stones
he moves with pauses,
much like commas in his stride;
hiccups in his personality

Finds a poplar and ascends
to elevated places,
where the tapered new growth bends
to the laws of weights and measures,
as he jumps to firmer oak,
exploration through its branches,
likened to a child in a toy store afternoon

Spring to pole with street below,
wire stretched out at your feet,
no hesitation does occur,
as the gray is set to meet

Delicately steps to task,
while forward motion takes one over road
with no circus crowd to cheer,
this performance thrill,
of yet another squirrel

The Journey

Stories in our lives to tell,
some of heaven and some of hell,
we traveled on from mother's womb,
found our music, played our tune

And in our years upon this earth
found our failures and our worth,
experienced the dead end road
and longer highways we were sold

Drawn to those who understood,
the knots we find inside the wood,
we're flawed but capable of love,
with some we fit, like hand in glove

Chapters read like poetry,
while others, like the raging sea,
compiled years and aged like wine,
some vinegar, some rather fine

Living, was a long, long test,
to learn about what's truly best,
not always with ourselves in mind,
but thoughtfulness and being kind

I hope I've passed, so far, so good,
this jackass even understood,
that it's about that goodness thing,
not what we take but what we bring

The Cricket's Band

Too long, I stayed in the woods one day,
then the day gave up the light
and before my eyes could blink three times,
I was greeted by the night

My ears heard sounds in the trees up high
and I trembled, lost, and cold,
for a little boy should be at home,
doing just what he's been told

Through fear, I prayed that the LORD would help
and that I would be OK,
when a cricket jumped up on a log
and acknowledged he would play

He was joined by many other friends,
who loved to perform and sing
and I learned to dance with fireflies,
as they joined me on the wing

The melodies were a sweet bouquet,
that removed my greatest fear,
all my worries stopped, and I didn't cry,
for I knew that GOD was near

The sun returned and the cricket bowed
and I thanked him for his time,
then I blinked one blink and he disappeared,
so, I walked home, safe, and fine

And although I looked for him at times,
as I grew up on the land,
our paths, they never crossed again,
but some nights, I hear his band

The Bird Feeder

The finch waits for me,
impatient, so bold,
from fence post to tree,
she flutters, to scold

"No food to consume,
we're all out of seed,"
she chatters her tune,
"It's our time to feed"

So on with the coat,
the gloves, and the hat,
the bucket I tote,
is where it's all at

A gourmet's delight,
oh, friends of the air,
fill up and take flight,
you haven't a care

A squirrel scampers by
for sunflower seeds,
the birds, with a sigh,
allow him his needs

"The snow's coming soon,"
the blue jay implies,
"It's cold but it's home,"
the cardinal cries

And all go their way,
as all eat their fill
and so goes the day,
from my windowsill

The Painted Horse

An earthen brown mixed evenly,
this canvas base was him,
with lighter shades, as weakened tea,
beneath his head and chin

A splash of snow across his face,
a splatter on his back,
on one hindquarter, just a trace,
on tail, just a track

Black markings with a hint of red,
throughout the creature's coat,
"He's like no other horse" they said,
in any saloon vote

Magnificent, in how he stood,
on high rock, near to me,
though we were one, I never could
claim ownership, you see

As sure as sunset colors come
and GOD remains at hand,
he ran the trails called "Freedom"
where no man owns the land

The Pond

On the grass lies morning dew,
a rabbit nibbles, ears alert,
I hear the birds, I kick the dirt
and climb the farmer's fence on through

Across the field, down the hill
and finally, so still, I see,
a place of pure tranquility,
with cattails as an added frill

Cane pole and my hand in bond,
I find my place along the shore,
I slip the bobber up some more
and swing the line into the pond

There is no pressing thing to do,
just watch the flight of dragonflies
and be a boy with watchful eyes,
observe a bright green frog or two

A chipmunk chatters a hello,
a red winged blackbird stops to chat,
my jeans are wet from where I sat
and still, I have no fish to show

I know a granddad bass is there,
asleep beneath a lily pad,
I wait, impatient, as a lad
and wonder if the fish could care

It matters not for life is sweet,
a beaver submarine's on by
and spotted by my eagle eye,
then tummy says, "It's time to eat!"

Adieu my pond, I make a wish
and say goodbye for I must leave,
it's lunchtime and my mom will grieve,
but I'll be back again, old fish

Whales

Song across the ocean
beckons to my ears,
the stories pass through centuries,
of whaling ships and tragedies
and how the salty waters came,
from many whale tears

Set the waves to motion,
listen to them cry,
the mighty whales slaughtered so,
as if their lives had naught to show,
they chant the question over time,
it's theirs to wonder why

Peace, their only notion,
hear them as they sing,
the sadness that has touched these lives,
harpooned and cut with boarding knives,
the decks of many ships ran red,
'tis such a horrid thing

Prayer, no healing lotion,
haunted melody,
they only wished to share this place
and occupy their fluid space,
enjoying life among the waves,
kind giants of the sea

Colors (the loss of someone)

Colors of a broken heart are many and a few,
for loss of someone special are the colors that they drew,
the tenderness that each one shared,
their truth, that times they were quite scared,
the empty page that's lost their laugh
and the fervor of their wrath

The song they sang which was their life,
one's confidence as well as strife,
all the colors that they knew,
colors of the rainbow too,
crystal white up in the night
however close or far,
we see their colors past the moon and in a twinkling star

Hope

A ship called Hope sits in the harbor waiting for its fill
it waits on souls who have a need and pray they have the will,
to make it through another day no matter dark, the sky,
it's there for us that understand, there's reason that we try

And when the ship is filled with those who want a better day,
they raise the gangway then the anchor, Hope is on its way,
sometimes the seas are rough at best, at times, a calm like peace
but Hope moves on the waters for to stop, all Hope would cease

It seems life's lived for granted, until life goes aground,
it sneaks up and surprises everyone without a sound
but there is always Hope dear friends, awaiting in the bay,
so, don't lose sight, in the dim light, know faith will guide your way

The Quenching (circa 1736)

On bended knee
I cup a moment of the stream in hand,
this part of what was once the whole,
now runs off through my fingers,
I lift it to my mouth,
invigorated by its texture,
as it moves along my throat
and I am satisfied,
I thirst no more

Brief time has me reflect its journey
down the mountain's side,
I reach again,
I splash my face,
then move on down the trail,
for adventure seeks companionship,
and I'm a lonely suitor
on the move

The Buck

An eight-point buck stood boldly in the middle of my way,
while our eyes locked for the moment, as dawn turned into day,
we measured distance, lay of land and where the wind did blow,
we contemplated forest, bush, and depth of fallen snow

I did not blink nor move a muscle waiting for the sun,
for I feared the mighty whitetail might break into full run,
he dropped his head to nibble on protruding chokecherry,
as sweat moved down my forehead where my eyes could barely see

I slowly raised my rifle as the light improved that morn,
I focused on my shot as spirit struggled through a storm,
the buck was trapped within my sights, but something was not right,
I couldn't bring myself to shoot and let the buck take flight

He bounded through the lower glen one cold December dream,
I was left with recollections of what my eyes had seen,
a creature so magnificent, who shared the forest wide,
was needed more by GOD that day than of some hunter's pride

Wayside

I watched one dozen geese
land easy on a pond,
wayside for their long enduring trek
and once again I was reminded
of the season's change,
how life comes by in chapters
that we never rearrange,
for in the order that they show
from spring bud to the white of snow,
we're gifted things,
each season brings,
both in our hands and mind,
from summer's long hot endless days
to winter's peace, we find

Saguaro

Cactus on an open plain
is left alone to hear the wind,
that blew along the flats
when generations passed before

Tumbleweeds roll quickly by
as this old sentry of the sand,
stands gallantly erect,
while sun and moon exchange the time

Signs appear as winter fades,
a change begins to show itself
and from the surface springs,
a flower for a moment's praise

Celebrating sacred life,
a desert bird is witness to,
the transformation that
has come and gone without a shout

Rain falls as a blessing thus,
a miracle that's rare at best,
the aftermath is but,
a quenching drink to hold one's own

What Bugs Me

The ordinary deerfly comes to mind,
a creature that's not very hard to find,
when I enjoy a walk on nature's path,
she sometimes comes to call, then spreads her wrath

I guess what really cuts and bothers me,
are not the circles 'round my thinking tree
but when the buzzing stops, to my surprise,
she never seems to sit where I have eyes

A lover of all life is what I claim
but there is nothing worse than that of pain,
so, if the little dear decides to land,
I'm most inclined to give a helping hand

Oh, creature of the forest air, be sweet,
move on and find another type of meat,
I'm willing to share life and all this space,
if you will only get out of my face

The Mountain

The mountain waits for every man
who would attempt the climb,
the challenge given, that one can,
move forth in such a staggered line,
as to progress beyond that place
where one has ceased to grow,
sure foot upon the mountain face,
conviction under every toe

Yon pinnacle at eye's own end,
so close, yet out of reach,
a lesson for each who ascend,
to come back down and teach

To My Son

Past recollections rise like water–colored memories,
we're on a mist filled winter lake around your seventh year,
the surface speckled bright with fishermen and ice shanties,
I hang this portrait in my mind and shed an old man's tear

Another vision comes from there, among our yesterdays,
you've wandered home from kindergarten frightened by it all,
I'm painting on the house, then realize your fearful gaze,
although you wish to stay, I send you packing at the crawl

Remembering the time that you and I lived on our own,
the puzzle of my life was scattered like a shattered pane,
in looking back, I wish that I had been a dad not stone,
at seventeen, warmth would have worked instead, the cold refrain

I can't undo the past but there are times I'd rearrange,
to reinvent life's canvas would be as a work of art,
with hindsight on my drawing table, I'd accept the change,
the charcoal sketches of my past do haunt this father's heart

Stone

I wonder of the mysteries a stone holds in its grasp,
of where it's been and what it's seen
through time which never waits,
if it was thrown in anger or to slay some passing beast,
perhaps it hid beneath the ground
and listened to above ground sound,
waiting to be lifted up, to where things turned to green
or smoothed its ragged edges in an old, cold, mountain stream

I'd like to hear the stories it might share if it could speak
and tell a tale of caves the stone had known,
it might have lived in valleys or on some volcanic ridge
or once was larger than today,
a remnant that broke fast away,
sitting still for years, watching seasons in review,
a part of everything that man does stumble through

Leaf Thoughts

I cannot grasp this tree too long,
for all the notes have left my song
and I wait upon the wind
for my release,
they say I'll drift awhile,
then tumble for a mile,
if no obstacles
will hold me and I cease

Whatever comes my way,
I am destined for a fall
but for now,
I stay here hanging by my stem,
connection to my host since I've known when,
the future isn't clear
but I've seen many splendid things,
from sun filled days,
to heavy rain,
to the song each songbird sings

The Farmer's Blessing

Weathered farm of many years,
balanced laughter with life's tears,
generations known to plow,
things are different right now

Snowflakes cover up the scars,
underneath a sea of stars,
what to plant that one could earn,
still, a family's concern

Getting harder each new day,
that the farmer finds his way,
growing season now has passed,
Christmas nears with arctic blast

A silent night just north of here,
a quiet scene we all hold dear,
we drive along the country road,
we pass the farmer, his abode

Reflecting on the cows and such,
know farmers never make that much,
remember when the meal's on,
the farmer starts before the sun

The Tree

I watch the tree outside my door,
it knows not peace, it knows not war,
it only seems to understand,
its needs are water and the land

It's not aware of Wall Street's woes
but of the coming of the snows,
it knows no prejudice or hate
but bares its leaves to dormant state

I've watched this tree for many years,
it stood by me through joy and tears,
each year it blossoms in the spring
and leaves return, cool shade they bring

At times I've wondered what it thought,
about us souls, so overwrought,
with our beliefs and steadfast ways,
our curse to self–destructive days

And through it all the tree remains,
past sunny days or pouring rains,
beyond the winter freeze, so cold
and still it stands, so tall, so bold

I watch this tree in my backyard
and wonder why our lives are hard,
in all of its simplicity,
there is a lesson in that tree

As You Mourn

May you know the peace of angels
when your heart is heavy, vision blurred,
may you comfort in GOD's silence
when you search but there's no word,
may you journey through the valley
with your loved ones as you mourn,
may you celebrate those taken
though your heart is sad and torn,
may you cherish times together
in the memories you share,
only love will guide you through this,
in that love, please know we care

Disease

Carried a mass in my mind and heart,
that never ceased when it had its start,
it worked on my body, a silent foe,
it made me sick, I would have you know

It brought me down to my bended knees,
for I was riddled with much dis ease,
grew on my organs and hurried my death,
brought me to where I was near my last breath

Then came the light of a different realm,
guiding my spirit was GOD at the helm,
telling me to put my great burden down,
filled me with love, with nary a sound

All of the sickness fled from my form,
it could not live without internal storm,
I stood erect like a beautiful tree,
for I had love in the fabric of me

Tales of the Woods

Faint whispers on the river fog
that hangs about cold mornings,
telling of long winters
when fire was a warm companion

A time when gold was the sun,
pinging off wet stones
and wind played the child,
as it frolicked the earth

I was but an observer,
taking in the beauty,
leaving it untouched,
for perfection cannot be improved

Shown the jewels of nature,
I prayed for their safekeeping,
then moved towards tomorrow
and things yet undiscovered

Early Evening Prayers

The remains of a day
takes one to the place of reflection
and to how the previous hours were made canvas
to the brush we spread our colors on,
leaving an impression
or a footprint on the earth and humanity alike,
in the positive or negative field of energy
surrounding us as we move through space,
knowing the gravity of the situation we are in

Being Thankful

What purpose being thankful when it's for another soul,
as it's easy to be thankful when it is our own true goal,
we are thankful when our team does win and takes the trophy home
but are we ok when it goes their way, or it sits like a gut stone?

I have come to understand that winning comes in many ways,
it's an abstract lesson hard to see but in greater realms it plays,
when we reach a place where all we are can relate to everything,
I believe it's then, one is rising to, where one hears the angels sing

Now I'm not quite there for the opposition still leaves me in knots
but I feel I'm on the learning path and great knowledge blooms in spots
but that fact that I've begun to see through the other people's eyes,
seems to startle me in a thankful way and is much to my surprise

Fresh Snow

Snow covered bridge over chasm,
undisturbed brilliance 'neath the sun,
almost a sadness to place a foot
undoing something grand
and though I know that I must go,
there's hesitation where I stand

In time, I make the journey
and mind hides from looking back,
for I wear it in my heart's place
this scene, without a track

Adaptation

The innovative man must change technique as time moves by
for what worked once to solve the task remembered only in a sigh,
the mind cries, computation, as we challenge all we know,
to find a better way to do the work and make a go

Of what we could do with our backs, our strength, a major tool
but strength fades like the waning day, believe or be the fool
but there are other avenues to search and finish up the chore,
we use the muscle on our necks to find another door

Sometimes it takes a pause in thought to equate each new move
but when the computation's done we find we're in the groove
and what was once impossible is now a memory
but now is not the time to gloat for new tasks wait for thee

Autumn on the Wind

I caught a faint impression on the wind,
'twas at the closing of the August moon,
as if to say, that summer had experienced its end
and autumn would appear one afternoon

Some flowers took to mourning right away,
some others fought to last until first frost,
the clouds moved slowly, colored white, off white and shades of gray,
great ships upon a blue sky, never lost

The fowl began to flock to each its kind,
they danced in air, filled full with bug and seed,
migration must have been fast on their thoughts and wings, I find,
warm weather was their most important need

The apples ripened on the apple trees
and soon the scent of cider and sweet pies,
the pumpkins, bright, with orange and greens came right up to our knees
and harvest brought GOD's bounty to our eyes

This Alaskan Way

Solace on the trapline,
silence in the snow laced birch and pine,
solo chickadee finds bits of food
provided by the marten kill,
the trap renewed, I move down to the next set

White Book; the name the Russians call it,
for in the reading comes the knowledge
of whom this wilderness is shared

A moose has fallen to a pack of wolves
some time ago,
a wolverine came by since then,
along with crows, mink, and mice,
all there to get a slice

Two dozen Ptarmigan hang out in the willows,
while the snowshoe hare holds steady,
near the ground,
eyes watching as I gather fur I've harvested
to keep me from the masses,
to help me in the day to day,
that I might live by sustenance, this Alaskan way

For Those Left Behind

Many fear their passing, to a realm of the unknown
but everything is energy and I'm told that GOD lives on
and although we slip the body, we remain a given soul,
that shines on in eternity, a brighter light, the goal

Departure is upending for all those left behind,
in later days we look around but there's no one there to find,
the brokenhearted who grieve on, have their family and friends,
for love is not something that stops, as it knows no ends

Get your house in order and pay all outstanding debts,
please cover all your wagers or never make those foolish bets,
live a life that is worth living, be forgiving and be kind,
for the ticket into heaven is a tender heart and mind

Quiet Times

At times I find the quiet in my day,
from the pace of work, beyond the joy of play,
to where distraction loses action
and calm's a centered place along the way
and most times, it is the salve that mends my fray

Rhythm of Life

Lake was calm, as the waters were asleep
and I stood quietly near shore as daylight entered peacefully,
a robust splash broke the membrane between the fluid and air,
as a great fish stirred from the depths of darkness
and I felt kin to the earth and all its miracles

Prayerful, I watched as the sun broke the horizon,
as an eagle lifted from roost, flying overhead, destination unknown,
colors danced the sky as I felt my heartbeat
and my breathing moved in the rhythm of life

Turning toward the cabin, there were eyes on me,
then the doe trotted toward the stream
and into the forest beyond

I found I was not alone but part of the greater picture
and peace was my companion for awhile

The Teacher

Somewhere beyond the last large hill,
beyond where rainbows form at will,
beyond the place where questions form,
and just beyond both cool and warm

There lived a comprehensive mind,
which seekers found real hard to find,
that mind sat easy in a case,
engulfed by body and a face

She went about the tasks at hand,
her job was but to understand,
she stored her findings in a book,
in reference, she'd take a look

The sun would come and then would go
and days would time away, you know,
now every now and then, you see,
a soul would come to be set free

The freedom came from thoughts involved,
when answers got their questions solved,
abilities she had like this,
to turn one's worries into bliss

Her life was not always this way
but came, by asking everyday
the owl, who so old and wise,
shared all he held behind his eyes

A mentor, guide, and teacher true,
the bird gave freely all he knew
and only asked, she'd be aware,
that knowledge was for her to share

Drifting

Sunlight paints the water's surface,
gently, rocks the wooden boat,
I lie in the womb, one purpose,
tranquil, as I onward float

Crossing liquid plains of motion,
no true destination seen,
half awake, in meditation,
between reality and dream

Shadows shade eyes, clouds are drifting,
much like me, they move in rhyme,
feelings that are so uplifting,
lost between the waves of time

Water laps the outer structure,
song of life is played like this,
heart and soul begin the rapture,
born again to find true bliss

Why We Sing

I've thought about existence all my many years
and those very misses that brought smiles and large tears,
I've wondered why I'm still around beneath this big blue sky
and figure GOD's still teaching me, the what, the where, and why

And so, I rise before the dawn to see what each day brings,
then wonder of the tawny sparrow and just why she sings,
when there are many birds around that stand out in the day
but each of us are just as worthy, GOD would proudly say

So, puckered lips upon my face are ready for to blow
and I'm inclined to whistle on for of this I truly know,
that when I'm called to the next realm and asked for who I am
I'll whistle, then be recognized, as noted in GOD's plan

The Fan

I shall not change my colors for convenience of the day,
nor wane in faith regardless of how my team does play,
I'll not find quick replacements in the shadow of defeat
and never, will I ever, let my loyalty retreat

Through the Rabbit's Eyes

The rain has passed
and I am 'neath the forest

I listen to the aftermath
of water moved by gravity,
from leaf to leaf
toward solace,
in the finding of the earth

A comfort has surrounded me,
emitted by the trees,
for as their roots replenish,
all are strengthened
and there's kindness
in the nature of the moment

New ferns unravel,
mushrooms sprout,
while slugs glide easy
over moss and ancient rocks
that sleep upon the ground

Small stream sings full
through winding chorus,
as the wind takes pause with me,
to share in what the rabbit
calls his home

Remembering Gratitude

Remember to have gratitude for without, the flower will not bloom
and death would kill the garden, soon a desert near high noon,
all decency might wither on a sandy, barren stage
and from within, where hearts are kept, might live an evil rage

But knowing this and understanding how we're led astray,
one might determine that there is a path which marks the way
and still, I'm prone to failure for my anger wilts the plants,
finding, I have gone a rambling with some nasty rants

So, when my mind awakens in the early morning hours,
I try to stay quite grounded from the ego's mighty towers,
I jot down what I'm grateful for like all my family,
my health, my friends, my life, and time,
the cloudy days and those that shine
and she, who puts up with this fool when storms do rock the sea,
my loving wife who shares my world and wonders about me

Mississippi Portrait

There's a morning mist rising on the secluded pond,
where frogs sit quietly in observation
and the dragonflies rest high upon the cattails,
ready for the sunlight, that they may take flight again

A mud turtle comes alive, releasing itself from a log,
slipping quickly into the waters below,
a heron landing disturbed its meditative state
and many onlookers have disappeared

The long–legged bird finds a comfortable spot
then freezes with head cocked slightly,
patiently waiting for breakfast to saunter by,
disturbed silt settles to the bottom of the pond in time

Silence of daybreak is shattered by the cawing of crows
but the heron is not moved by their song,
fire ants patrol near the water looking for the deceased,
while a field mouse moves through the wild grass

High above, in a branch of a water oak, a hawk waits,
her eye on anything that moves beneath her domain,
somewhere high a cloud slips overhead,
as two bluebirds search for housing on a summer's day

Divorce

What cause shall die today
by love's adieu,
what pain shall fade away
from me or you

Who'll rise above the dust
and truly gain,
then simply readjust
those hurts that reign

Where goes the broken heart
when left to mourn,
to live one's life apart,
in time…reborn

What prize shall we procure
as we both flee,
I hope you've won, I'm sure,
it was not me

If Man Would Pray

If one would pray, what would it be,
fame and fortune, celebrity
or might one pray for streams and lakes,
with cleaner waters for our sakes,
abundance of our foul and fish
to feed the world, more than a wish,
that vegetation fills our need,
replanting all that gives us seed,
for cleaner air and clearer skies,
no longer hurting lungs and eyes,
perhaps, we'd pray for peace on Earth
for each soul born has equal worth,
no selfishness to what we pray,
for all might see a brighter day

Sister

I claim one sister after me,
which I'm the oldest, as you see,
we shared our years of childhood,
as family and siblings should

As I went my way down the street
and she, with girlfriends, found her beat,
sometimes we gathered for a meal,
as normal children, no big deal

At times she was my nemesis
and told on me, that naughty Sis,
two parents, sister and plus me,
dysfunctional for all to see

I joined the Army at eighteen,
lost track of her while in my dream,
we were in touch but not as close,
we gathered, then said, "adios!"

I moved out East for many years,
we talked at times through joy and tears,
retired in the south a while,
then came home to my sister's smile

We bonded in our later days
became closer in our ways,
I always loved my sister true,
and she assured, she always knew

The Understanding

We understand so little of this life
as days go swiftly by
but maybe we were here to learn
GOD's lessons or just try,
no academic grade is given as we go
but as man climbs his mountain,
each step is closer, don't you know,
to seeing through the eyes of GOD
and knowing what to do,
the right thing sometimes swallows hard
in truth, for me and you
and as our time runs through the hourglass,
'tis easier to pray, I find,
while things are less important
than the act of being kind

Art of Forgiving

Forgiveness is a measure of wisdom,
for it closes the door on a hurt shared
by the actions of two entities
and becomes the salve of healing
for those wounded in the tangle of life
and if not remedied,
it festers like gangrene,
causing discomfort until addressed
and put to rest

The Race

The turtle moves along in life at such a given pace
he's quick to note his memory, of the one, great race,
where patience overtook his foe by "steady as a rock"
and while the hare relaxed and napped, he still was on the clock

Smart turtle kept his focus and remained a steadfast force,
he moved along with fortitude to finish up the course
and when the flippant rabbit awoke in record time,
the turtle had the race secured just past the finish line

A Song

Each one of us a song played throughout our days,
a melody so fashioned, it orchestrates our ways,
there is no right or wrong to it
no gain nor is a deficit,
just notes which play our written music as we're given birth
and the score is noted down as we discover worth

Symphony,
written forth for you and me,
music illustrates the water's flow
and as we're mainly water,
it records where we have been and where we'll go

Grandpa

I remember grandpa's hat,
always hanging by the door
and on head, just how it sat
when he took me to the store

Penny candy was my treat
as he spoke of yesterday,
as we walked on down the street,
hand in hand, our special way

I remember grandpa's pants,
kind of loose and hanging so
and they bounced when he would dance,
striped suspenders gave them go

Large plaid shirts with rolled up sleeves,
old brown shoes that had no shine,
hair, that blessed his ears and eaves,
said his friend was Father Time

I remember grandpa's heart,
warm and tender, full of grace,
always tried to do his part
when someone was on their face

Always had kind things to say,
never had an enemy,
told me, GOD had made each day
and to thank GOD constantly

I remember grandpa's house,
looking back on memories,
like the little field mouse
that he'd bless with bits of cheese

And the flowers he would pick,
for my grandma, with a smile,
always cheerful, seldom sick,
'til he walked his final mile

Shine

There's a bluebird flying slowly past my window,
I can see a little teardrop in his eye
and I wonder if he'll still be sad tomorrow,
see, the forecast calls for clouds across the sky

There's a willow that is weeping in the field,
it's her nature to be sad most every day,
still, I wonder if the tears bring forth a yield,
if for nothing else, to cheer her in some way

There's a mantis that is praying for some reason
and just lately, he's been praying all the time,
well, I wonder if he prays to change the season,
so, the willow and the bluebird start to shine

There are people like the friends that I have mentioned
and they weep, for they have sadly lost their way,
hope the weatherman would get a new invention,
that would spread the clouds and bring a sunny day

www.ingramcontent.com/pod-product-compliance
Lightning Source LLC
LaVergne TN
LVHW021550080426
835510LV00019B/2456